Jumpstarters for Algebra

Short Daily Warm-ups for the Classroom

By
WENDI SILVANO

COPYRIGHT © 2005 Mark Twain Media, Inc.

ISBN 1-58037-295-3

Printing No. CD-404022

Mark Twain Media, Inc., Publishers
Distributed by Carson-Dellosa Publishing Company, Inc.

Table of Contents

Introduction to the Teacher 1

Real Numbers 2

    Skills Covered: Real number line; ordering numbers; reciprocals; order of operation; absolute value; comparing numbers; addition, subtraction, multiplication, and division of real numbers; properties of real numbers

Algebraic Expressions 5

    Skills Covered: Variables, exponents, coefficients, like and unlike terms, simplifying and evaluating expressions, translating phrases to algebraic expressions, open sentences, solution sets

Linear Equations and Inequalities 9

    Skills Covered: Simplifying expressions; addition, subtraction, multiplication, and division properties; percents; solving linear equations; solving linear inequalities

Polynomials 14

    Skills Covered: Exponents and scientific notation; multiplication and division of monomials; addition, subtraction, multiplication, and division of polynomials

Factoring 18

    Skills Covered: Greatest common factors and monomial factors of polynomials, factoring trinomials, factoring the difference of squares, factoring by grouping

Rational Expressions 22

    Skills Covered: Simplifying rational expressions, multiplying and dividing rational expressions, least common denominator, adding and subtracting rational expressions, ratios and proportions

Linear Equations and Inequalities in Two Variables 26

    Skills Covered: Rectangular coordinate system, graphing linear equations, linear equations in two variables, slope-intercept, equations of lines

Systems of Linear Equations and Inequalities 30

    Skills Covered: Solving systems of linear equations by graphing, elimination, and substitution; solving systems of linear inequalities

Square Roots and Radicals 33

    Skills Covered: Simplifying square root expressions; addition, subtraction, multiplication, and division of square roots; equations involving square roots; Pythagorean Theorem

Quadratic Equations 37

    Skills Covered: Solving quadratic equations by factoring, by the square root method, by completing the square, and by the quadratic formula

Answer Keys 39

# Introduction to the Teacher

It is important for students to review and practice the skills they gain as they learn algebra. Revisiting math skills several days after they are first learned is a helpful way to reinforce those skills.

This book is intended to offer the teacher and parent short warm-up activities to help the student practice the skills that are taught in the classroom. There are five mini-activities on each page of this book that can be used at the beginning of class to help students focus on algebra for the day. The activities use all of the basic skills of algebra from real numbers to quadratic equations.

Each page may be copied and cut apart, so that the individual sections can be used as warm-up activities for each day of the week. The teacher could also give each student the entire page to keep in a three-ring binder to use as assigned. Another option would be to make a transparency of the page to be done as whole-class activities or for the students to copy. Please be aware that students will need scratch paper to complete some of the warm-ups.

Algebra Warm-ups:
Real Numbers

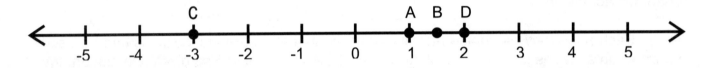

Name/Date _____

Real Numbers 1

Give the coordinate of each point on the number line.

A. _____   B. _____   C. _____   D. _____

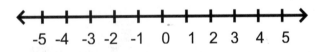

Name/Date _____

Real Numbers 2

Graph these numbers on the number line.

A. (-3)   B. (+$3\frac{1}{2}$)   C. (-4.5)   D. (+$\frac{1}{4}$)

$$\longleftarrow \overset{}{\underset{-5 \; -4 \; -3 \; -2 \; -1 \; \; 0 \; \; 1 \; \; 2 \; \; 3 \; \; 4 \; \; 5}{|\;|\;|\;|\;|\;|\;|\;|\;|\;|\;|}} \longrightarrow$$

Name/Date _____

Real Numbers 3

List each set of real numbers in order from least to greatest.

a. (4, -2, -$\frac{3}{4}$, $1\frac{1}{3}$, 0)

_____

b. (4.6, $\sqrt{25}$, -2.8, 4.10, -3)

_____

Name/Date _____

Real Numbers 4

Place >, <, or = on each line to make each statement true.

a. -2 _____ 4   b. 5.38 _____ 5.3

c. $1\frac{1}{2}$ _____ 1.5   d. -3.1 _____ -3.6

Name/Date _____

Real Numbers 5

Simplify.

a. -(-4) _____

b. (-[-($\frac{1}{5}$)]) _____

c. | 16 | _____

d. | -9.1 | _____

Algebra Warm-ups:
Real Numbers

Name/Date _____

Real Numbers 6

Find each difference.

a. -(16) − (-5) = _____   b. (-36) − (14) = _____

c. $\frac{2}{3} - (-\frac{1}{3})$ = _____   d. 16 − (-4) = _____

e. (3.5) − (-1.1) − (2.6) = _____

Name/Date _____

Real Numbers 7

Find each product.

a. (-4) (5) = _____   b. (12) (6) = _____

c. (2.1) (-4.3) = _____   d. $(-\frac{2}{3})$ $(-\frac{4}{5})$ _____

e. (3) (6) (-5) = _____

Name/Date _____

Real Numbers 8

Find each quotient.

a. -81 ÷ 3 = _____   b. $-\frac{36}{9}$ = _____

c. $-\frac{1}{2} ÷ (-\frac{2}{3})$ = _____   d. 0 ÷ 116 = _____

e. 8.75 ÷ (-0.5) = _____

Name/Date _____

Real Numbers 9

Find the difference.
In January, the average daily low temperature in Fairbanks, Alaska, is -18°F. In July, it is 52°F. How many degrees difference is there between the average daily low temperatures of January and July? _____

Name/Date _____

_____

Real Numbers 10

Find each sum.

a. -4 + 7 = _____

b. -3 + (-4) = _____

c. 286 + (-153) = _____

d. -622 + (-304) = _____

e. (1.2) + (3.3) + (-1.6) =

_____

f. $(-\frac{2}{5}) + (-\frac{1}{3}) + (\frac{3}{5})$ = _____

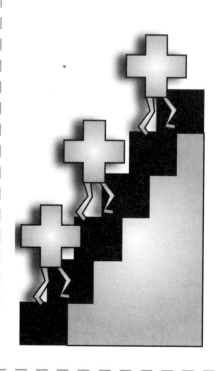

3

Algebra Warm-ups:
Real Numbers

Name/Date _____

Real Numbers 11

Mark "T" for true or "F" for false for each statement.

_____ a. -6 + 4 = 4 + (-6)

_____ b. 8 − 12 = 12 − 8

_____ c. 6 + (14 − 8) = (6 + 14) − 8

_____ d. 9 ÷ 3 = 3 ÷ 9

_____ e. 2(3 + 5) = 2(3) + 2(5)

Name/Date _____

Real Numbers 12

Write the reciprocal of each number.

a. -3 _____   b. $\sqrt{21}$ _____

c. $\frac{3}{4}$ _____   d. -2 _____

e. $\frac{19}{8}$ _____   f. $\frac{12}{\sqrt{7}}$ _____

Name/Date _____

Real Numbers 13

Number these rules to show the order of operations.

_____ Evaluate expressions with exponents.

_____ Do all additions and subtractions in order from left to right.

_____ Do all operations within parentheses.

_____ Do all multiplications and divisions in order from left to right.

Name/Date _____

Real Numbers 14

Simplify.

a. $18 − 3 \cdot 4 + 6 ÷ 3$ _____

b. $3(2 + 5) - 2^2$ _____

c. $4(6 + 8 − 3 + 1)$ _____

Name/Date _____

Real Numbers 15

Simplify.

a. $\{20 - [3(1 + 3)]\} \cdot 2$ _____

b. $3^3 + (14 − 8) \cdot 2$ _____

c. $(4^2 + 2^2) ÷ 5$ _____

Algebra Warm-ups:
Algebraic Expressions

Name/Date _____

Algebraic Expressions 1

Evaluate each expression if $n = 12$.

a. $n + 15$ _____

b. $50 - n$ _____

c. $7n$ _____

d. $\dfrac{n}{4}$ _____

Name/Date _____

Algebraic Expressions 2

Evaluate each expression if $a = 3$, $b = 5$, and $c = 2$.

a. $3abc$ _____

b. $\dfrac{1}{2}a + b$ _____

c. b^c _____

Name/Date _____

Algebraic Expressions 3

Evaluate each expression if $p = \frac{1}{4}$ and $r = \frac{1}{2}$.

a. $p + r$ _____

b. $r - p$ _____

c. pr _____

d. $\dfrac{p}{r}$ _____

Name/Date _____

Algebraic Expressions 4

Write an algebraic expression that could answer each question if n is Dan's age now.

a. What was Dan's age 3 years ago?

_____

b. What age will Dan be in 8 years?

_____

c. How many years until Dan is 50?

_____

Name/Date _____

Algebraic Expressions 5

Write an algebraic expression for each phrase.

a. Some number n increased by 8 _____

b. The difference of 12 and s _____

c. Three less than 4 times a number t _____

d. g divided by h _____

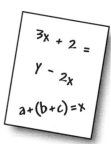

Algebra Warm-ups:
Algebraic Expressions

Name/Date _____

_____

Algebraic Expressions 6

Evaluate each expression if $x = 2$ and $y = 3$.

a. $x^2 y$ _____

b. $x^3 y^2$ _____

c. $x^2 + y^2$ _____

d. $-(xy)^2$ _____

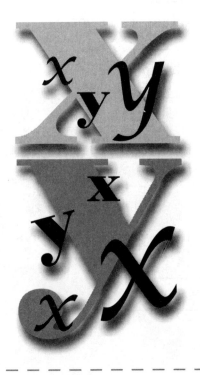

Name/Date _____

Algebraic Expressions 7

Evaluate each expression.

a. x^4 if $x = 2$ _____

b. r^3 if $r = 3$ _____

c. m^3 if $m = -1$ _____

d. $n^2 - n$ if $n = 4$ _____

Name/Date _____

Algebraic Expressions 8

Evaluate each expression if $a = 3$, $b = 4$, and $c = -2$.

a. $-b + c^2$ _____

b. $(c - a)^2$ _____

c. $a^2 (b + c)^2$ _____

d. $-(3a + 2c)^3$ _____

Name/Date _____

Algebraic Expressions 9

Evaluate each expression if $x = 2$ and $y = -3$.

a. $x^2 + y^2 + 1$ _____

b. $2x^2 - 3x + 5$ _____

c. $3x^2 + 2y$ _____

d. $x^3 - 2y$ _____

Name/Date _____

Algebraic Expressions 10

Evaluate each expression if $a = -2$, $b = 6$, and $c = 4$.

a. $\dfrac{a^3 + c^2}{bc}$ _____

b. $-b + a^2 (3c - a)$ _____

c. $b^2 \div (c^2 - a)$ _____

Algebra Warm-ups:
Algebraic Expressions

Name/Date _____

Algebraic Expressions 11

For each expression, tell whether the terms are *like* or *unlike*.

  a. $4s + 8$ _____

  b. $2a^2b + 3ab^2$ _____

  c. $3xy^2 + 2xy^2$ _____

  d. $2pq^2r - pq^2r$ _____

Name/Date _____

Algebraic Expressions 12

Write the coefficient of each term.

a. $6x^2$ _____   b. y _____

c. $5y^3$ _____   d. $10z^5$ _____

e. $18a^4b^2$ _____

Name/Date _____

Algebraic Expressions 13

Simplify.

  a. $2n + 4n + 5n^2 + 3n^2$ _____

  b. $5x^2y + 2x^2y - 3xy$ _____

  c. $-6 + 3(2b - 4) + 3b$ _____

  d. $4a^3b + 3ab^3 + 2a^3b + 6ab^3$ _____

Name/Date _____

Algebraic Expressions 14

Simplify.

  a. $5(ab^2 - 2ab) + 3(ab - ab^2)$ _____

  b. $\frac{1}{2}(4x + 2y) + \frac{1}{3}(12x - 6y)$ _____

  c. $3(g^3 - h) + 4(g^3 - 8)$ _____

Name/Date _____

_____

Algebraic Expressions 15

Simplify.

  a. $2n + 4n$ _____

  b. $-4y - 3y$ _____

  c. $7 + 2t + 4$ _____

  d. $12b^2 - 4b^2$ _____

  e. $3(x + 4) - 6$ _____

  f. $6x^3y - 3x^3y + 4xy$

  _____

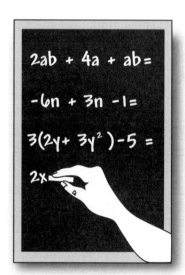

Algebra Warm-ups:
Algebraic Expressions

Name/Date _____

Algebraic Expressions 16

Translate each phrase into an algebraic expression. (Use *n* to represent a variable.)

a. Five more than three times a number _____

b. Four times the sum of a number and six _____

c. Two less than eight times a number squared _____

Name/Date _____

Algebraic Expressions 17

Write an algebraic expression for one un-known in terms of the other. (Use *g* to represent the girls and *b* to represent the boys.)

   a. There are four more boys than girls in class. _____

   b. If the girls' team wins one more game, they will have won twice as many games as the boys.

   _____

Name/Date _____

Algebraic Expressions 18

Find the solution set of each sentence. The replacement set is {-1,0,1}.

   a. $k + 3 = 3$ _____

   b. $m + 1 = 0$ _____

   c. $y + 1 \le 1$ _____

   d. $2n > 2$ _____

Name/Date _____

Algebraic Expressions 19

A stereo costs $110. John paid $35 down and made 5 equal payments on the stereo. Write an algebraic equation that could be used to find out how much his payments were.

_____

Name/Date _____

Algebraic Expressions 20

Andrea's new coat costs $25 more than twice as much as her old one. The new coat costs $105. Write an algebraic equation that could be used to determine how much her old coat cost.

_____

8

Algebra Warm-ups:
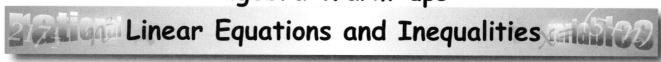
Linear Equations and Inequalities

Name/Date _____

Linear Equations and Inequalities 1

Tell which operation you would perform on each side of the equation to get x alone on one side.

    a. $x + 3 = 7$ _____

    b. $-4 = -1 + x$ _____

    c. $x - 6 = 10$ _____

    d. $x - (-12) = 15$ _____

Name/Date _____

Linear Equations and Inequalities 2

Solve.

    a. $a - 4 = 24$ _____

    b. $m + 3 = 18$ _____

    c. $r + 11 = 22$ _____

    d. $12 + s = -10$ _____

Name/Date _____

Linear Equations and Inequalities 3

Is the given number a solution for the equation?

	Given Number	Equation	
a.	3	$x + 3 = 5$	_____
b.	2	$3y + 6 = 12$	_____
c.	-5	$\dfrac{3v - 5}{4} = -5$	_____

Name/Date _____

Linear Equations and Inequalities 4

Solve.

    a. $b - (-4) = 10$ _____

    b. $-3.4 + r = -9.5$ _____

    c. $5 = x + 2\frac{1}{3}$ _____

    d. $b - 3.12 = 5.23$ _____

Name/Date _____

Linear Equations and Inequalities 5

Write and solve an algebraic equation to answer the following.

If a number n is decreased by 32, it equals 11. Find n.

_____

Algebra Warm-ups:
Linear Equations and Inequalities

Name/Date _____

Linear Equations and Inequalities 6

What must be done to each side of the equation so the variable will be alone on one side?

    a. $6x = 42$ _____

    b. $\frac{2}{3}m = 1$ _____

    c. $-18 = -3y$ _____

Name/Date _____

Linear Equations and Inequalities 7

Solve.

    a. $-5t = 30$ _____

    b. $2x = 14$ _____

    c. $\frac{x}{7} = -4$ _____

    d. $\frac{3}{5}p = 12$ _____

Name/Date _____

Linear Equations and Inequalities 8

Solve.

    a. $1.25x = 5$ _____

    b. $\frac{2}{3}a = 4$ _____

    c. $\frac{s}{5} = 10$ _____

    d. $-3.5b = 14$ _____

Name/Date _____

Linear Equations and Inequalities 9

Write an algebraic equation for each word sentence, and then solve.

a. The quotient of 30 and a number n equals 6. _____

b. The product of 9 and a number c equals 27. _____

Name/Date _____

Linear Equations and Inequalities 10

Is the given number a solution for the equation?

Given Number		Equation	
a.	5	$6x = 42$	_____
b.	7	$\frac{14}{b} = 2$	_____
c.	-3	$\frac{5m + 3}{6} = -2$	_____

Algebra Warm-ups:
Linear Equations and Inequalities

Name/Date _____

Linear Equations and Inequalities 11

Solve.

    a. $4m + 8 = 20$ _____

    b. $2x - 4 = 6$ _____

    c. $b + 11 = 4$ _____

    d. $\frac{2}{3}k + 7 = 13$ _____

Name/Date _____

Linear Equations and Inequalities 12

Solve.

    a. $3(x - 4) = 12$ _____

    b. $\frac{1}{4}(a - 16) = 16$ _____

    c. $2y - 15 = -1$ _____

    d. $\frac{2c - 6}{2} = 9$ _____

Name/Date _____

Linear Equations and Inequalities 13

Complete each sentence.

    a. If $x + 7 = 9$, then $11 - x =$ _____

    b. If $4y + 2 = 14$, then $2y + 1 =$ _____

    c. If $3b + 4 = 19$, then $6b =$ _____

    d. If $2c - 1 = 5$, then $c + 8 =$ _____

Name/Date _____

Linear Equations and Inequalities 14

Solve each problem by writing and solving an equation.

a. Ten less than three times x is 50. Find x.

_____

b. The sum of n and five times n equals 12.

_____

Name/Date _____

_____

Linear Equations and Inequalities 15

The formula to find the area of a triangle is $A = \frac{1}{2}bh$.

a. What is the area (A) if $b = 6$ and $h = 5$?

_____

b. What is the height (h) if $b = 4$ and $A = 16$?

_____

c. What is the base (b) if $h = 4$ and $A = 12$?

_____

Algebra Warm-ups:
Linear Equations and Inequalities

Name/Date _____

_____

Linear Equations and Inequalities 16

Solve. The circumference of a circle can be found with the formula $C = 2\pi r$.

a. Find C if $\pi = 3.14$ and $r = 10$.

_____

b. Find r if $C = 94.2$ and $\pi = 3.14$.

_____

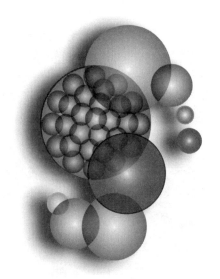

Name/Date _____
Linear Equations and Inequalities 17

Use the distributive property to find each product.

a. $6(n - 4)$ _____

b. $(5 + d)3$ _____

c. $25(4 + 3s)$ _____

d. $3(a + b)$ _____

Name/Date _____
Linear Equations and Inequalities 18

Solve.

a. $a + (a + 4) + (2a - 3) = 13$ _____

b. $2(y - 3) = 12$ _____

c. $8(m - 1) = 8$ _____

d. $-2(4x - 3) = -14$ _____

Name/Date _____
Linear Equations and Inequalities 19
Solve.

a. What is 8% of 98? _____

b. 6 is what percent of 24? _____

c. 40% of what number is 60? _____

d. What is 15.5% of 50? _____

Name/Date _____
Linear Equations and Inequalities 20
Solve.

a. $3a - 8 = -6 + a$ _____

b. $4x - 10 = x - 16$ _____

c. $-5b = 3(4 - 3b)$ _____

d. $2x + 4(x - 2) = -(2x - 8)$ _____

Algebra Warm-ups:
Linear Equations and Inequalities

Name/Date _____

Linear Equations and Inequalities 21

Solve and state the solution set.

a. $|2a + 7| = 9$ _____

b. $|\frac{1}{3}b - 2| = 4$ _____

c. $|y - 4| > 6$ _____

d. $|2g - 9| \geq 1$ _____

Name/Date _____

Linear Equations and Inequalities 22

Solve.

a. $2y - 1 = -3(2 + y)$ _____

b. $-3(x - 2) + 4 = 4(x + 1)$ _____

c. $5u - 14 = -5 + 8u$ _____

Name/Date _____

Linear Equations and Inequalities 23

Circle the sentence that best describes the graph.

a. $x \geq -2$ b. $x = -2$ c. $x < -2$

d. $x > -2$ e. $x \leq -2$

-4 -3 -2 -1 0 1 2 3 4

Name/Date _____

Linear Equations and Inequalities 24

Solve.

a. $4y + 6 < 2y - 6$ _____

b. $5x + 2 - 4x \geq 3$ _____

c. $8c < 56$ _____

d. $\frac{3}{4}b \geq -18$ _____

Name/Date _____

Linear Equations and Inequalities 25

Solve.

a. $3(m - 1) - 4 \leq 2 - 4(2 - m)$ _____

b. $-3 + 2r \neq 9 - 2r$ _____

c. $\frac{2}{3}b < -8$ _____

d. $-2.5x \leq 12.5$ _____

13

Algebra Warm-ups:
Polynomials

Name/Date _____

Polynomials 1

Simplify.

a. 3^3 _____   b. 8^0 _____

c. $(-2)^{-2}$ _____   d. $8^6 \div 8^4$ _____

Name/Date _____

Polynomials 2

Rewrite each number in scientific notation.

a. 645 _____

b. 0.0023 _____

c. 48726.5 _____

d. $(3 \cdot 10^4)(4 \cdot 10^5)$ _____

Name/Date _____

Polynomials 3

Simplify. Assume that no variable equals 0.

a. $\dfrac{d^7}{d^4}$ _____   b. $\dfrac{c^2}{c^5}$ _____

c. $\dfrac{2ab^7}{5a^4}$ _____   d. $\dfrac{4x^2y^5}{2x^6y^2}$ _____

Name/Date _____

Polynomials 4

Simplify. Assume that no variable equals 0.

a. $(w^5)^6$ _____   b. $\left(\dfrac{-r}{s^3}\right)^8$ _____

c. $\left(\dfrac{4x}{5y}\right)^2$ _____   d. $\left(\dfrac{4u^2v}{-3u^5v^2}\right)^2$ _____

Name/Date _____

_____

Polynomials 5

Simplify.

a. $(b^6)(b^3)$

_____

b. $(2n^2m)(4n^4m^3)$

_____

c. $(6x^3y)(3x^4y^4)$

_____

d. $(3a^{2x})(a^{3x})$

_____

Algebra Warm-ups:
Polynomials

_____

Polynomials 6

State the degree in each polynomial.

a. $3n$

_____

b. $4x^2 - 2x + 6$

_____

c. $-10ab^3c^5$

_____

d. $5u^2v^2 + 8u^2v^2 + 3uv - 2$

_____

Polynomials 7

Write each monomial in factored form.

a. $-2b^3$ _____

b. $3^2x^5y^2$ _____

c. $-4a^2b^3$ _____

d. $(-x)^4$ _____

Polynomials 8

Rewrite each polynomial in descending order of the exponents with respect to x.

a. $2x - 5x^3 + 7 - x^4$ _____

b. $4x^3y^2 - x^8 + 2 - 3x^6y$ _____

c. $-6 + 8x^3y^4 - 3x^2y - 2x^5y^5$ _____

Polynomials 9

Solve.

a. $(3x^2 - 4x + 6) + (2x - 2x^2 + 2)$

_____

b. $(2m^3 - 4m^2 + m - 6) + (2m^2 + 6m^3 + 9)$

_____

Polynomials 10

Add these polynomials.

a. $(3x^3 + 2x^2 - 4x - 8) + (x^2 - 3x + 9)$

_____

b. $(3a^2 - 6a - 4) + (a^2 + 9 - 7a^3 + 2a)$

_____

Algebra Warm-ups:
Polynomials

Name/Date _____

Polynomials 11

Subtract.

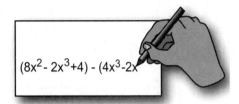

$(8x^2 - 2x^3 + 4) - (4x^3 - 2x$

a. $(7e^3 - 3e^2 + 9e + 1) - (3e^3 - e^2 + 5e - 7)$ _____

b. $(6b^3 + 3b^2 - b - 6) - (b^2 - 8b + 9)$ _____

Name/Date _____

Polynomials 12

Subtract.

a. $(r - 3r^2 + r^3 - 7) - (2r^3 - 4r + 6)$

_____

b. $(2y^4 + y^2 - y) - (y^2 + 2y)$

_____

Name/Date _____

Polynomials 13

Add or subtract as indicated.

a. $(6x + 5y - 3z) - (4x - 3y + 2z)$

_____

b. $(3a + 2b + 4) + (7a - b + 3)$

_____

Name/Date _____

Polynomials 14

If n is an integer, write an algebraic expression to find the sum of n and the next four consecutive integers. Then simplify.

_____

_____

Name/Date _____

Polynomials 15

Multiply.

a. $(-4b^4)(5b^5)$ _____

b. $3x^2y(4x + 2y - r)$ _____

c. $7m^2(m^3 - 3m^4 + 5m^2)$ _____

16

Algebra Warm-ups:
Polynomials

Name/Date _____

Polynomials 16

Multiply.

a. $(x + 5)(x - 8)$ _____

b. $(3a - 2)(5 + 6a)$ _____

c. $(2p - 3r)(4p + r)$ _____

Name/Date _____

Polynomials 17

Multiply.

a. $(2n - 3m)^2$ _____

b. $(y^2 + 2y + 1)(y - 5)$ _____

c. $(d - 2)(d - 2)(d - 2)$ _____

Name/Date _____

Polynomials 18

Multiply.

a. $(g + 5)(g - 5)$ _____

b. $(2a - b)^2$ _____

c. $(4h^5 + 3i^4)(4h^5 - 3i^4)$ _____

Name/Date _____

Polynomials 19

Divide.

a. $(16r^2 - 8r + 12) \div 4$ _____

b. $(12a^4 - 6a^2 + 4a) \div 2a$ _____

c. $(20n^5 + 10n^3 - 15n^2 + 5n) \div 5n$ _____

Name/Date _____

_____

Polynomials 20

Divide.

a. $(2c^2 - 3c - 2) \div (c - 2)$

_____

b. $(2y^2 + 3y - 20) \div (y + 4)$

_____

c. $(6x - x - 12) \div (2x - 3)$

_____

Algebra Warm-ups:
Factoring

Name/Date _____

Factoring 1

Write each as the product of its factors by using exponents.

a. $2 \cdot 2 \cdot 2 \cdot 2$ _____

b. $3 \cdot 3 \cdot 5 \cdot 5 \cdot 5$ _____

c. $2 \cdot 5 \cdot 3 \cdot 3 \cdot 3$ _____

d. $11 \cdot 11 \cdot 11 \cdot 11 \cdot 11 \cdot 13 \cdot 13$ _____

Name/Date _____

Factoring 2

Write the prime factorization of each number. (Use exponents for repeated factors.)

a. 70 _____

b. 135 _____

c. 338 _____

d. 1,000 _____

Name/Date _____

Factoring 3

Factor.

a. $3p + 15$ _____

b. $2r + 7r^2$ _____

c. $16x + 12y$ _____

d. $4b^2 - 8b$ _____

Name/Date _____

Factoring 4

Factor.

a. $2m^3n - 12m^2n^4$

_____

b. $5x^2y - 15x^3y^3$

_____

c. $4g^2h + 8g^2h^2 + 12gh$

_____

Name/Date _____

Factoring 5

Factor.

a. $9a^2b^4 - 54a^5b^3$

_____

b. $2x^3 - 6x^2 + 10x$

_____

c. $-15c^3d^4 - 35c^4d^5 - 55c^2d^4$

_____

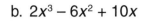

F
A
C
T
O
R
S

Algebra Warm-ups:
Factoring

Name/Date _____

Factoring 6

Solve.

a. $x^2 + 12x + 11$

_____

b. $48 + 19c + c^2$

_____

c. $m^2 - 9m + 14$

_____

d. $b^2 - 18b + 32$

_____

Name/Date _____

Factoring 7

Factor.

a. $y^2 + 4y + 3$ _____

b. $7 + 8j + j^2$ _____

c. $k^2 + 14k + 13$ _____

d. $s^2 - 12s + 35$ _____

Name/Date _____

Factoring 8

Factor.

a. $x^2 - 16xy + 48y^2$ _____

b. $r^2 - 27rs + 72s^2$ _____

c. $u^4 - 16u^2 + 28$ _____

d. $a^2 + 32ab + 60b^2$ _____

Name/Date _____

Factoring 9

Factor.

a. $y^2 - y - 12$ _____

b. $x^2 + 6x - 7$ _____

c. $b^2 + 2b - 3$ _____

d. $r^2 - 13r - 30$ _____

Name/Date _____

Factoring 10

Factor.

a. $a^2 - ab - 2b^2$ _____

b. $m^2 - 14mn - 32n^2$ _____

c. $x^2 - 8xy - 20y^2$ _____

d. $r^4 - 23r^2 - 50$ _____

Algebra Warm-ups:
Factoring

Name/Date _____

Factoring 11

Factor.

a. $3a^2 - 22a - 16$ _____

b. $2b^2 + 7b + 5$ _____

c. $3x^2 + 17x + 20$ _____

d. $5y^2 - 13y - 6$ _____

Name/Date _____

Factoring 12

Factor.

a. $m^2 - 12m + 36$ _____

b. $t^2 + 20t + 100$ _____

c. $x^2 + 8x + 16$ _____

d. $r^2 + 26r + 169$ _____

Name/Date _____

Factoring 13

Factor.

a. $25a^2 + 10a + 1$ _____

b. $49c^2 + 14c + 1$ _____

c. $mn^3 - m^3n$ _____

d. $9h^{12} + 6h^6 + 1$ _____

Name/Date _____

Factoring 14
Factor by grouping.

a. $15x^2 + 12x + 6x^3$

_____

b. $5(y-3) + 2(y-3) - 3(y-3)$

_____

c. $21a - 21b + 15a - 15b$

_____

d. $mr + nr + ms + ns$

_____

Name/Date _____

Factoring 15
Factor.

a. $y^2 - 5x - 25 + xy$

_____

b. $ab + ac - 3b - 3c$

_____

c. $mp - 2m + 3np - 6n$

_____

d. $2pq - 5qr - 4p + 10r$

_____

Algebra Warm-ups:
Factoring

Name/Date _____

Factoring 16

Solve by factoring.

a. $n^2 + 4n = 0$ _____

b. $3p^2 - 6p = 0$ _____

c. $5h^2 + 15h = 0$ _____

Name/Date _____

Factoring 17

Solve by factoring.

a. $a^2 - 8a + 15 = 0$ _____

b. $r^2 - 3r - 18 = 0$ _____

c. $2b^2 + 13b - 24 = 0$ _____

Name/Date _____

Factoring 18

Solve by factoring.

a. $x^2 - 6x + 9 = 0$ _____

b. $10a^3 - 29a^2 - 21a = 0$ _____

c. $y^5 - 10y^3 + 9y = 0$ _____

Name/Date _____

Factoring 19

Write an algebraic equation and solve it to find
two consecutive integers whose product is 56.

_____

Name/Date _____

_____

Factoring 20

Solve by factoring.

a. $2b(b - 3) = 0$

_____

b. $(2c - 6)(c + 6) = 0$

_____

c. $(4y - 3)(y + 5) = 0$

_____

Algebra Warm-ups:
Rational Expressions

Name/Date _____

_____

Rational Expressions 1

State the value(s) of the variable for which each expression is undefined.

a. $\dfrac{3}{m-2}$

_____

b. $\dfrac{2r}{(r-5)(3r-2)}$

_____

c. $\dfrac{a+b}{2x+1}$

_____

d. $\dfrac{c-4}{c^2-16}$

_____

Name/Date _____

Rational Expressions 2

Simplify and state the values for which the expression is undefined.

a. $\dfrac{3a}{12a^2}$ _____

b. $\dfrac{7x-14}{x-2}$ _____

c. $\dfrac{r+2}{5r^2+7r-6}$ _____

d. $\dfrac{24y+18}{36}$ _____

Name/Date _____

Rational Expressions 3

Simplify and state the values for which the expression is undefined.

a. $\dfrac{2y^2+9y-5}{y^2+10y+25}$

_____

b. $\dfrac{9+11z+2z^2}{z^2-10z-11}$

_____

Name/Date _____

Rational Expressions 4

Multiply. Assume all denominators do not equal 0.

a. $\dfrac{5s}{3s^2} \cdot \dfrac{4}{s^2y}$ _____

b. $\dfrac{12xy^2}{5y^3z^2} \cdot \dfrac{5xz}{3x}$ _____

c. $\dfrac{2n+4}{3n-9} \cdot \dfrac{6n-18}{4n+20}$ _____

Name/Date _____

Rational Expressions 5

Multiply. Assume all denominators do not equal 0.

a. $\dfrac{h-5}{4h+6} \cdot \dfrac{6h+9}{3h-15}$

b. $\dfrac{2y+4}{6y-8} \cdot \dfrac{y-5}{y+2}$

_____

c. $\dfrac{3b-15}{4b-2} \cdot \dfrac{20b-10}{15b-75}$ _____

Algebra Warm-ups:
Rational Expressions

Name/Date _____

Rational Expressions 6

Multiply. Assume all denominators do not equal 0.

a. $\dfrac{3m^2 - 10m - 8}{2m} \cdot \dfrac{-2m - 8}{m^2 - 16}$ _____

b. $\dfrac{b^2 - 3b - 10}{(b-2)^2} \cdot \dfrac{b-2}{b-5}$ _____

Name/Date _____

Rational Expressions 7

Divide.

a. $\dfrac{2}{x} \div \dfrac{3y}{2x}$ b. $\dfrac{a}{b} \div \dfrac{b^2}{a^3}$

_____   _____

c. $\dfrac{9}{n} \div \dfrac{3r}{4n}$ _____

Name/Date _____

Rational Expressions 8

Divide.

a. $\dfrac{2x^2}{y^2} \div \dfrac{14x}{3y}$ b. $\dfrac{c+5}{c+14} \div (c+5)$ c. $\dfrac{s^2 - 9}{s^2 - 2s - 24} \div \dfrac{s-3}{s-6}$

_____   _____   _____

Name/Date _____

Rational Expressions 9

Divide.

a. $\dfrac{5e^2 + 10e - 15}{e^2 - 6x + 5} \div \dfrac{2e^2 + 7e + 3}{4e^2 - 8e - 5}$

_____

b. $\dfrac{a^2 - a - 20}{a^2 + 7a + 12} \cdot \dfrac{a^2 - 10a + 25}{a^2 + 6a + 9}$

_____

Name/Date _____

Rational Expressions 10

Find the least common denominator.

a. $\dfrac{-3}{2a^3b}$ and $\dfrac{4a}{6a^3b^5}$ _____

b. $\dfrac{5}{12x^3y}$ and $\dfrac{-3}{10xy^2}$ _____

Algebra Warm-ups:
Rational Expressions

Name/Date _____

Rational Expressions 11

Find the lowest common denominator.

a. $\dfrac{1}{5mn}$ and $\dfrac{3n}{2m}$ _____

b. $\dfrac{7}{d^2 - 4}$ and $\dfrac{3}{d - 2}$ _____

Name/Date _____

Rational Expressions 12

Find the lowest common denominator and write the equivalent expressions with the LCD as denominator.

$\dfrac{5}{9x^2y}$ and $\dfrac{2x}{3y^2}$

a. LCD _____

b. Equivalent expressions _____

Name/Date _____

Rational Expressions 13

Add or subtract.

a. $\dfrac{9}{2b} + \dfrac{3}{2b}$ _____

b. $\dfrac{2p}{p + 1} + \dfrac{5p}{p + 1}$ _____

c. $\dfrac{5x}{x + 2} - \dfrac{x - 8}{x + 2}$ _____

Name/Date _____

Rational Expressions 14

Add or subtract.

a. $\dfrac{5b + 1}{25 - b^2} + \dfrac{5}{b + 5}$ _____

b. $\dfrac{3}{2c} + \dfrac{2}{4c^2} - \dfrac{1}{c}$ _____

c. $\dfrac{4}{2y + 8} - \dfrac{y}{5y + 20}$ _____

Name/Date _____

Rational Expressions 15

Add or subtract.

a. $\dfrac{2}{4r^2} - \dfrac{2r + 3}{6r^3}$ _____

b. $\dfrac{m}{m + 2} + \dfrac{5}{m - 6}$ _____

c. $\dfrac{5u - 2}{u^2 + u - 20} - \dfrac{3}{u + 5} + \dfrac{u}{u - 4}$ _____

Algebra Warm-ups:
Rational Expressions

Name/Date _____

Rational Expressions 16

Simplify.

a. $2 + \dfrac{1}{e}$ _____

b. $5 - \dfrac{7}{y}$ _____

c. $3i - \dfrac{i+1}{i}$ _____

Name/Date _____

Rational Expressions 17

Simplify.

a. $\dfrac{2a-1}{a+2} + a$

_____

b. $\dfrac{\dfrac{k}{2} - \dfrac{k}{3}}{\dfrac{k}{6} + \dfrac{2}{3}}$

_____

Name/Date _____

Rational Expressions 18

Are these ratios equal?

a. $\dfrac{2}{5} = \dfrac{6}{15}$ _____

b. $\dfrac{4}{8} = \dfrac{9}{15}$ _____

c. $4:5 = 8:15$ _____

d. $2:8 = 12:48$ _____

Name/Date _____

Rational Expressions 19

Solve these ratios.

a. $\dfrac{5}{6} = \dfrac{30}{y}$

b. $\dfrac{12d}{28} = \dfrac{15}{7}$

c. $\dfrac{4}{a+4} = \dfrac{2}{3a+2}$

_____   _____   _____

Name/Date _____

_____

Rational Expressions 20

A bag contains 10 red marbles, 4 green marbles, and 9 blue marbles. If you reached into the bag and took out 1 marble, what is the probability that ...

a. it will be red?

_____

b. it will not be red?

_____

c. it will be blue or red?

_____

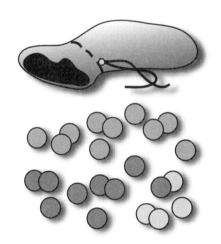

Algebra Warm-ups:
Linear Equations and Inequalities in Two Variables

Name/Date _____

_____

Linear Equations and Inequalities in Two Variables 1

Determine if each ordered pair is a solution of the equation $x + 3y = 6$.

a. (3, 1) _____

b. (4, 2) _____

c. (9, -1) _____

d. (0, 2) _____

e. (-2, 2) _____

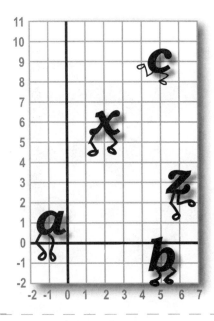

Name/Date _____

Linear Equations and Inequalities in Two Variables 2

Name the point that is the graph of each ordered pair.

a. (-3, -4) _____

b. (2, -3) _____

c. (2, 2) _____

d. (-1, 1) _____

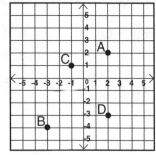

Name/Date _____

Linear Equations and Inequalities in Two Variables 3

Graph the ordered pairs and connect the points.

a. (1, 0)

b. (3, 2)

c. (-2, 3)

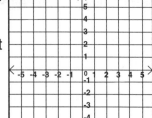

Name/Date _____

Linear Equations and Inequalities in Two Variables 4

Make a solution table for the equation. Then graph the equation $y = 9 - 3x$.

x	y

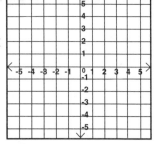

Name/Date _____

Linear Equations and Inequalities in Two Variables 5

Determine the missing coordinate of each ordered pair solution of $y = x + 6$.

a. (0, y) _____   b. (2, y) _____

c. (x, 0) _____   d. (x, 4) _____

Algebra Warm-ups:
Linear Equations and Inequalities in Two Variables

Name/Date _____

Linear Equations and Inequalities in Two Variables 6

Find the x and the y intercepts of the graph of each equation.

$$x + y = 7 \qquad 2x + y = 8 \qquad 3x - y = 6$$

x intercept _____   _____   _____

y intercept _____   _____   _____

Name/Date _____

Linear Equations and Inequalities in Two Variables 7

On your own paper, graph the equation $x - y = 5$ using at least three points.

Name/Date _____

Linear Equations and Inequalities in Two Variables 8

On your own paper, graph the equation $2x + 2y = 8$ using at least three points.

Name/Date _____

Linear Equations and Inequalities in Two Variables 9

On your own paper, graph the equation $4y - x = 2$ using at least three points.

Name/Date _____

_____

Linear Equations and Inequalities in Two Variables 10

Solve each equation for y.

a. $x + y = 8$

   _____

b. $4x = 2y - 1$

   _____

c. $3(x - 1) - 4(y + 5) = 12$

   _____

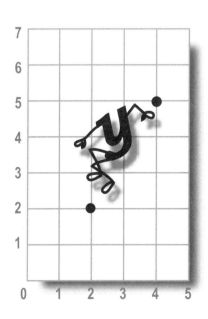

Algebra Warm-ups:
Linear Equations and Inequalities in Two Variables

Name/Date _____

Linear Equations and Inequalities in Two Variables 11

Find the slope of a line that contains the given points.

a. A (-2, 3) B (2, 1) _____

b. C (6, 7) D (1, 3) _____

c. E (-1, 3) F (2, 4) _____

Name/Date _____

Linear Equations and Inequalities in Two Variables 12

Find the slope of a line that contains the given points.

a. A (1, 3) B (2, 3)_____

b. C (5, -2) D (4, 3) _____

c. E (3, 8) F (1, 4) _____

Name/Date _____

Linear Equations and Inequalities in Two Variables 13

Find the value of the missing coordinate using the given slope.

A (x, 0) and B (3, 4), slope = 2

_____

Name/Date _____

Linear Equations and Inequalities in Two Variables 14

Find the slope and the y intercept of the line for the given equation.

$$4x + 3y = 12$$

slope _____

y intercept _____

Name/Date _____

Linear Equations and Inequalities in Two Variables 15

Find the slope and the y intercept of the line for the given equation.

$$8x - y = 2$$

slope _____

y intercept _____

Algebra Warm-ups:
Linear Equations and Inequalities in Two Variables

Name/Date _____

_____

Linear Equations and Inequalities in Two Variables 16

Write an equation in slope-intercept form that contains the given points.

A (5, 6) B (6, 9)

_____

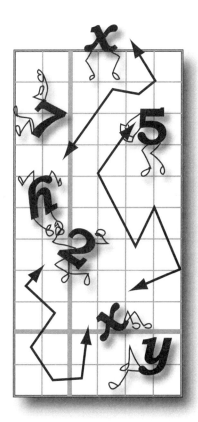

Name/Date _____

Linear Equations and Inequalities in Two Variables 17

Write an equation of a line in standard form given a point and the slope.

point (0, 3)   slope: $-\frac{1}{2}$

_____

Name/Date _____

Linear Equations and Inequalities in Two Variables 18

Write an equation of a line in standard form given a point and the slope.

point (2, 6)   slope: $\frac{3}{2}$

_____

Name/Date _____

Linear Equations and Inequalities in Two Variables 19

Graph the inequality $x \geq 2$.

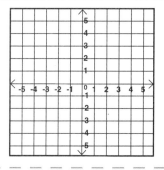

Name/Date _____

Linear Equations and Inequalities in Two Variables 20

Graph the inequality $y \geq -x + 3$.

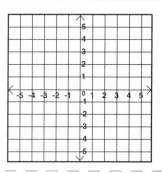

Algebra Warm-ups:
Systems of Linear Equations and Inequalities

Name/Date _____

Systems of Linear Equations and Inequalities 1

On your own paper, solve by graphing:

$$\begin{cases} x - 2y = 1 \\ x + 2y = 1 \end{cases}$$

Name/Date _____

Systems of Linear Equations and Inequalities 2

Without graphing, describe the graph and tell the number of solutions.

$$\begin{cases} 8x - 6y = 2 \\ 6x - 8y = 2 \end{cases}$$ _____

_____

Name/Date _____

Systems of Linear Equations and Inequalities 3

Solve by substitution.

a. $\begin{cases} y = 2x \\ 7x - y = 35 \end{cases}$ b. $\begin{cases} 3x - y = 17 \\ y + 2x = 8 \end{cases}$

_____   _____

Name/Date _____

Systems of Linear Equations and Inequalities 4

Solve by substitution.

a. $\begin{cases} 3x + 2y = 4 \\ y = x - 3 \end{cases}$ b. $\begin{cases} y = 3x + 1 \\ y = 6x - 1 \end{cases}$

_____   _____

Name/Date _____

_____

Systems of Linear Equations and Inequalities 5

Solve by substitution.

a. $\begin{cases} x - y = 0 \\ x + y = 2 \end{cases}$

_____

b. $\begin{cases} 3x + 2y = 9 \\ x + y = 3 \end{cases}$

_____

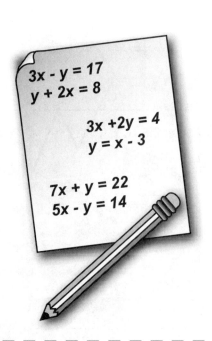

$3x - y = 17$
$y + 2x = 8$

$3x + 2y = 4$
$y = x - 3$

$7x + y = 22$
$5x - y = 14$

30

Algebra Warm-ups:
Systems of Linear Equations and Inequalities

Name/Date _____

Systems of Linear Equations and Inequalities 6

Solve by elimination.

a. $\begin{cases} x + y = 10 \\ x - y = 12 \end{cases}$
b. $\begin{cases} -x + y = 4 \\ x + y = 8 \end{cases}$

_____ _____

Name/Date _____

Systems of Linear Equations and Inequalities 7

Solve by elimination.

a. $\begin{cases} x + y = 0 \\ x - y = -6 \end{cases}$
b. $\begin{cases} 7x + y = 22 \\ 5x - y = 14 \end{cases}$

_____ _____

Name/Date _____

Systems of Linear Equations and Inequalities 8

Solve by elimination.

a. $\begin{cases} 2x = y + 1 \\ 2y - x = 1 \end{cases}$
b. $\begin{cases} 2x - 5y = 17 \\ 6x = 5y + 1 \end{cases}$

_____ _____

Name/Date _____

Systems of Linear Equations and Inequalities 9

Write an equation for each word sentence.

a. A number n is four more than two times a number m. _____

b. A number a is half as much as three less than a number b. _____

Name/Date _____

Systems of Linear Equations and Inequalities 10

Write an equation for each word sentence.

a. Six years from now, Steve will be 4 years older than twice Roy's age now.

_____

b. The amount of money in dimes is half the amount of money in quarters.

_____

Algebra Warm-ups:
Systems of Linear Equations and Inequalities

Name/Date _____

_____

Systems of Linear Equations and Inequalities 11

Write a system of linear equations for the problem, and then solve.

Pam has 26 coins in nickels and quarters. Together they are worth $3.10. How many of each coin does she have?

_____

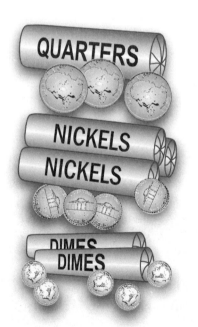

Name/Date _____

Systems of Linear Equations and Inequalities 12

Write a system of linear equations for the problem, and then solve.

The sum of two numbers is 36. If the smaller number is subtracted from the larger number, the difference is 4.

_____

Name/Date _____

Systems of Linear Equations and Inequalities 13

Write a system of linear equations for the problem, and then solve.

Together José and Dan sold 137 candy bars for the fundraiser. If José sold 10 fewer than twice as many as Dan, how many did each of them sell?

_____

Name/Date _____

Systems of Linear Equations and Inequalities 14

Write a system of linear equations for the problem, and then solve.

Ella is 3 years older than Marta. Four years ago, Ella was twice as old as Marta. How old are they both now?

_____

Name/Date _____

Systems of Linear Equations and Inequalities 15

Write a system of linear equations for the problem, and then solve.

David is 3 times as old as Alex. In three years, the sum of their ages will be 54. How old is each of them now?

_____

Algebra Warm-ups:
Square Roots and Radicals

Name/Date _____

Square Roots and Radicals 1

Find the square roots.

a. $\sqrt{49}$ _____   b. $\pm\sqrt{0.81}$ _____

c. $-\sqrt{\frac{1}{16}}$ _____   d. $\sqrt{900}$ _____

Name/Date _____

Square Roots and Radicals 2

Find the square roots.

a. $\pm\sqrt{576}$ _____   b. $\sqrt{0.0025}$ _____

c. $-\sqrt{-(2-11)}$ _____   d. $-\sqrt{1.96}$ _____

Name/Date _____

Square Roots and Radicals 3

Simplify.

a. $\sqrt[4]{81}$ _____   b. $\sqrt[5]{32}$ _____

c. $\sqrt[3]{64}$ _____   d. $\sqrt[3]{-125}$ _____

Name/Date _____

Square Roots and Radicals 4

Simplify.

a. $\sqrt{72}$ _____   b. $\sqrt{108}$ _____

c. $\sqrt{44}$ _____   d. $\sqrt{90}$ _____

Name/Date _____

_____

Square Roots and Radicals 5

Simplify.

a. $\sqrt{24}$

_____

b. $\sqrt{150}$

_____

c. $\sqrt{48}$

_____

d. $\sqrt{1,000}$

_____

Algebra Warm-ups:
Square Roots and Radicals

Name/Date _____

Square Roots and Radicals 6

Evaluate for the given value of the variable, and then simplify, if possible.

a. $\sqrt{a-7}$, $a = 15$ b. $\sqrt{b+3}$, $b = 25$

_____   _____

c. $\sqrt{3c+6}$, $c = 7$ _____

Name/Date _____

Square Roots and Radicals 7

Simplify. Assume all variables represent non-negative real numbers.

a. $\sqrt{9a^3b^4}$ _____   b. $\sqrt{\frac{50}{49}}$ _____

c. $\frac{9}{\sqrt{5}}$ _____   d. $\sqrt{\frac{25}{81}}$ _____

Name/Date _____

Square Roots and Radicals 8

Simplify. Assume all variables represent non-negative real numbers.

a. $4\sqrt{11} + 3\sqrt{11}$ _____

b. $8\sqrt{15} - 4\sqrt{15}$ _____

c. $\sqrt{6} - 4\sqrt{6}$ _____

Name/Date _____

Square Roots and Radicals 9

Simplify. Assume all variables represent non-negative real numbers.

a. $-5\sqrt{x} + \sqrt{9x}$ _____   b. $\sqrt{16r} - \sqrt{r}$ _____

c. $4\sqrt{12} + 5\sqrt{27}$ _____

Name/Date _____

_____

Square Roots and Radicals 10

Simplify.

a. $\sqrt{x^4y}$ _____

b. $\sqrt{81y^9}$ _____

c. $\sqrt{b^4c^6}$ _____

d. $\sqrt{88r^4}$ _____

Algebra Warm-ups:
 ## Square Roots and Radicals

Name/Date _____

_____

Square Roots and Radicals 11

Simplify. Assume variables represent non-negative real numbers.

a. $11\sqrt{5} - 2\sqrt{20} + 4\sqrt{45}$

_____

b. $\sqrt{9n} - \sqrt{16n} + \sqrt{25n}$

_____

Name/Date _____

Square Roots and Radicals 12

Simplify. Assume variables represent non-negative real numbers.

a. $3\sqrt{36y} + \sqrt{100y} - 2\sqrt{64y}$ _____

b. $\sqrt{b} - 7\sqrt{b} + 6\sqrt{b}$ _____

Name/Date _____

Square Roots and Radicals 13

Multiply and simplify.

a. $(\sqrt{5})(\sqrt{10})$ _____

b. $(2\sqrt{3})(-3\sqrt{2})$ _____

c. $(\sqrt{\frac{9}{2}})(\sqrt{\frac{2}{3}})$ _____

Name/Date _____

Square Roots and Radicals 14

Multiply and simplify.

a. $(\sqrt{2} + 3)(\sqrt{2} - 3)$ _____

b. $\sqrt{7}(4 + \sqrt{7})$ _____

c. $(4\sqrt{n})^2$ _____

Name/Date _____

Square Roots and Radicals 15

Rationalize the denominator and simplify.

a. $\sqrt{\frac{1}{2}}$ _____   b. $\frac{-2\sqrt{3}}{\sqrt{5}}$ _____

c. $\frac{3\sqrt{2}}{4\sqrt{32}}$ _____

Algebra Warm-ups:
Square Roots and Radicals

Name/Date _____

Square Roots and Radicals 16

Rationalize the denominator and simplify.

a. $\dfrac{4\sqrt{3}}{2\sqrt{8}}$ b. $\sqrt{\dfrac{8}{y}}$ c. $\sqrt{\dfrac{24x^3}{6x}}$

_____   _____   _____

Name/Date _____

Square Roots and Radicals 17

Solve these radical equations.

a. $\sqrt{g} = 8$ _____   b. $\sqrt{\dfrac{b}{3}} = 2$ _____

c. $\sqrt{2y-1} - 3 = 1$ _____

Name/Date _____

Square Roots and Radicals 18

Solve these radical equations.

a. $\sqrt{s-2} = 3$ b. $\sqrt{\dfrac{2n}{3}} + 5 = 7$

_____   _____

c. $\sqrt{4r^2 - 27} = r$ _____

Name/Date _____

Square Roots and Radicals 19

Use the Pythagorean Theorem ($a^2 + b^2 = c^2$) to find the missing lengths.

a. $a = 5$, $c = 13$, $b = ?$ _____

b. $b = 4$, $c = 5$, $a = ?$ _____

c. $a = \sqrt{3}$, $b = 1$, $c = ?$ _____

Name/Date _____

_____

Square Roots and Radicals 20

Use the Pythagorean Theorem ($a^2 + b^2 = c^2$) to find the distance between each pair of points.

a. R (1, 2), S (4, -2)

_____

b. B (6, 2), C (6, -8)

_____

Algebra Warm-ups:
Quadratic Equations

Name/Date _____

Quadratic Equations 1

Solve by factoring. Express all radicals in simplest form.

a. $u^2 - u - 12 = 0$

_____

b. $4a^2 - 9a = 0$

_____

c. $6b^2 = 17b - 12$

_____

Name/Date _____

Quadratic Equations 2

Solve by factoring. Express all radicals in simplest form.

a. $3d^2 - 10 = 13d$ _____

b. $7c^2 - 12c = 0$ _____

c. $5x^2 + 13x = 6$ _____

Name/Date _____

Quadratic Equations 3

Solve by the square root method. Express all radicals in simplest form.

a. $r^2 = \sqrt{\dfrac{4}{25}}$ _____   b. $36b^2 = 18$ _____

c. $2r^2 = 16$ _____

Name/Date _____

Quadratic Equations 4

Solve by the square root method. Express all radicals in simplest form.

a. $g^2 - 49 = 0$ _____

b. $h^2 - 169 = 0$ _____

c. $25x^2 - 81 = 0$ _____

Name/Date _____

Quadratic Equations 5

Solve by the square root method. Express all radicals in simplest form.

a. $(b - 1)^2 = 9$ _____

b. $3g^2 - 36 = 0$ _____

c. $(7e + 3)^2 = 16$ _____

Algebra Warm-ups: Quadratic Equations

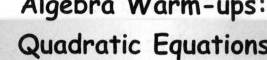

Name/Date _____

_____

Quadratic Equations 6

Solve by completing the square. Express all radicals in simplest form.

a. $a^2 - 2a - 8 = 0$

_____

b. $c^2 + 10c + 3 = 0$

_____

c. $4r^2 - 12r = -9$

_____

$b^2 + 5b + 6 = 0$

Name/Date _____

Quadratic Equations 7

Solve by completing the square. Express all radicals in simplest form.

a. $2x^2 - 2x - 2 = 0$ _____

b. $b^2 + 12b = 45$ _____

c. $a^2 - 4a + 2 = 0$ _____

Name/Date _____

Quadratic Equations 8

Solve by using the quadratic formula.

a. $2a^2 - 3a - 5 = 0$ _____

b. $b^2 + 5b + 6 = 0$ _____

Name/Date _____

Quadratic Equations 9

Solve by using the quadratic formula.

a. $x^2 - 3x - 10 = 0$ _____

b. $r^2 - 3r + 6 = 4$ _____

Name/Date _____

Quadratic Equations 10

Solve each quadratic equation by any appropriate method.

a. $4y^2 - 20 = 0$ _____

b. $s^2 - 4s = -3$ _____

Answer Keys

Real Numbers 1 (p. 2)
A = 1; B = 1.5; C = -3; D = 2

Real Numbers 2 (p. 2)

Real Numbers 3 (p. 2)
a. $(-2, -\frac{3}{4}, 0, 1\frac{1}{3}, 4)$
b. $(-3, -2.8, 4.10, 4.6, \sqrt{25})$

Real Numbers 4 (p. 2)
a. <   b. >   c. =   d. >

Real Numbers 5 (p. 2)
a. 4   b. $\frac{1}{5}$ c. 16   d. 9.1

Real Numbers 6 (p. 3)
a. -11   b. -50   c. 1
d. 20   e. 2

Real Numbers 7 (p. 3)
a. -20   b. 72   c. -9.03
d. $\frac{8}{15}$ e. -90

Real Numbers 8 (p. 3)
a. -27   b. -4   c. $\frac{3}{4}$
d. 0   e. -17.5

Real Numbers 9 (p. 3)
70°

Real Numbers 10 (p. 3)
a. 3   b. -7   c. 133   d. -926
d. 2.9   e. $-\frac{2}{15}$

Real Numbers 11 (p. 4)
a. T   b. F   c. T
d. F   e. T

Real Numbers 12 (p. 4)
a. $-\frac{1}{3}$ b. $\frac{1}{\sqrt{21}}$ c. $\frac{4}{3}$

d. $-\frac{1}{2}$ e. $\frac{8}{19}$ f. $\frac{\sqrt{7}}{12}$

Real Numbers 13 (p. 4)
2, 4, 1, 3

Real Numbers 14 (p. 4)
a. 8   b. 17   c. 48

Real Numbers 15 (p. 4)
a. 16   b. 39   c. 4

Algebraic Expressions 1 (p. 5)
a. 27   b. 38   c. 84   d. 3

Algebraic Expressions 2 (p. 5)
a. 90   b. 6.5   c. 25

Algebraic Expressions 3 (p. 5)
a. $\frac{3}{4}$ b. $\frac{1}{4}$ c. $\frac{1}{8}$ d. $\frac{1}{2}$

Algebraic Expressions 4 (p. 5)
a. $n - 3$ b. $n + 8$ c. $50 - n$

Algebraic Expressions 5 (p. 5)
a. $n + 8$ b. $12 - s$ c. $4t - 3$ d. $\frac{g}{h}$

Algebraic Expressions 6 (p. 6)
a. 12   b. 72   c. 13   d. -36

Algebraic Expressions 7 (p. 6)
a. 16   b. 27   c. -1   d. 12

Algebraic Expressions 8 (p. 6)
a. 0   b. 25   c. 36   d. -125

Algebraic Expressions 9 (p. 6)
a. 14   b. 7   c. 6   d. 14

Algebraic Expressions 10 (p. 6)
a. $\frac{1}{3}$ b. 50   c. 2

Algebraic Expressions 11 (p. 7)
a. unlike   b. unlike   c. like   d. like

Algebraic Expressions 12 (p. 7)
a. 6   b. 1   c. 5   d. 10
e. 18

Algebraic Expressions 13 (p. 7)
a. $6n + 8n^2$ b. $7x^2y - 3xy$
c. $9b - 18$ d. $6a^3b + 9ab^3$

Algebraic Expressions 14 (p. 7)
a. $2ab^2 - 7ab$ b. $6x - y$
c. $7g^3 - 3h - 32$

Algebraic Expressions 15 (p. 7)
a. $6n$ b. $-7y$ c. $2t + 11$
d. $8b^2$ e. $3x + 6$ f. $3x^3y + 4xy$

Algebraic Expressions 16 (p. 8)
a. $3n + 5$ b. $4(n + 6)$ c. $8n^2 - 2$

Algebraic Expressions 17 (p. 8)
a. $b = g + 4$ b. $g + 1 = 2b$

Algebraic Expressions 18 (p. 8)
a. $\{0\}$ b. $\{-1\}$ c. $\{-1, 0\}$ d. $\{\}$

Algebraic Expressions 19 (p. 8)
$5n + 35 = 110$

Algebraic Expressions 20 (p. 8)
$2x + 25 = 105$

Linear Equations and Inequalities 1 (p. 9)
a. Subtract 3.   b. Add 1.
c. Add 6.   d. Subtract 12.

Linear Equations and Inequalities 2 (p. 9)
a. 28   b. 15   c. 11   d. -22

Linear Equations and Inequalities 3 (p. 9)
a. no   b. yes   c. yes

Linear Equations and Inequalities 4 (p. 9)
a. 6   b. -6.1   c. $2\frac{2}{3}$ d. 8.35

Linear Equations and Inequalities 5 (p. 9)
$n - 32 = 11,\ n = 43$

Linear Equations and Inequalities 6 (p. 10)
a. Divide by 6.   b. Multiply by $\frac{3}{2}$.
c. Divide by -3.

Linear Equations and Inequalities 7 (p. 10)
a. -6   b. 7   c. -28   d. 20

Linear Equations and Inequalities 8 (p. 10)
a. 4   b. 6   c. 50   d. -4

Linear Equations and Inequalities 9 (p. 10)
a. $\frac{30}{n} = 6,\ n = 5$ b. $9c = 27,\ c = 3$

Linear Equations and Inequalities 10 (p. 10)
a. no   b. yes   c. yes

Linear Equations and Inequalities 11 (p. 11)
a. 3   b. 5   c. -7   d. 9

Linear Equations and Inequalities 12 (p. 11)
a. 8   b. 80   c. 7   d. 12

Linear Equations and Inequalities 13 (p. 11)
a. 9   b. 7   c. 30   d. 11

Linear Equations and Inequalities 14 (p. 11)
a. $3x - 10 = 50,\ x = 20$
b. $n + 5n = 12,\ n = 2$

Linear Equations and Inequalities 15 (p. 11)
a. $A = 15$ b. $h = 8$ c. $b = 6$

Linear Equations and Inequalities 16 (p. 12)
a. $C = 62.8$ b. $r = 15$

Linear Equations and Inequalities 17 (p. 12)
a. $6n - 24$ b. $15 + 3d$ c. $100 + 75s$
d. $3a + 3b$

Linear Equations and Inequalities 18 (p. 12)
a. 3   b. 9   c. 2   d. 2.5

Linear Equations and Inequalities 19 (p. 12)
a. 7.84   b. 25%   c. 150   d. 7.75

Linear Equations and Inequalities 20 (p. 12)
a. 1   b. -2   c. 3   d. 2

Linear Equations and Inequalities 21 (p. 13)
a. $\{1, -8\}$ b. $\{18, -6\}$
c. $y > 10,\ y < -2$ d. $g \le 4,\ g \ge 5$

Linear Equations and Inequalities 22 (p. 13)
a. -1   b. $\frac{6}{7}$ c. -3

Linear Equations and Inequalities 23 (p. 13)

a

Linear Equations and Inequalities 24 (p. 13)

a. $y < -6$ b. $x \geq 1$ c. $c < 7$
d. $b \geq -24$

Linear Equations and Inequalities 25 (p. 13)

a. $m \geq -1$ b. $r \neq 3$ c. $b < -12$
d. $x \geq -5$

Polynomials 1 (p. 14)

a. 27   b. 1   c. $\frac{1}{4}$ d. 64

Polynomials 2 (p. 14)

a. $6.45 \cdot 10^2$ b. $2.3 \cdot 10^{-3}$
c. $4.87265 \cdot 10^4$ d. $1.2 \cdot 10^{10}$

Polynomials 3 (p. 14)

a. d^3 b. $\dfrac{1}{c^3}$ c. $\dfrac{2b^7}{5a^3}$ d. $\dfrac{2y^3}{x^4}$

Polynomials 4 (p. 14)

a. w^{30} b. $\dfrac{r^8}{s^{24}}$ c. $\dfrac{16x^2}{25y^2}$ d. $\dfrac{16}{9u^6v^2}$

Polynomials 5 (p. 14)

a. b^9 b. $8n^6m^4$ c. $18x^7y^5$ d. $3a^{5x}$

Polynomials 6 (p. 15)

a. 1   b. 2   c. 9   d. 4

Polynomials 7 (p. 15)

a. $-2 \cdot b \cdot b \cdot b$
b. $3 \cdot 3 \cdot x \cdot x \cdot x \cdot x \cdot x \cdot y \cdot y$
c. $-4 \cdot a \cdot a \cdot b \cdot b \cdot b$
d. $(-x)(-x)(-x)(-x)$

Polynomials 8 (p. 15)

a. $-x^4 - 5x^3 + 2x + 7$
b. $-x^8 - 3x^6y + 4x^3y^2 + 2$
c. $-2x^5y^5 + 8x^3y^4 - 3x^2y - 6$

Polynomials 9 (p. 15)

a. $x^2 - 2x + 8$ b. $8m^3 - 2m^2 + m + 3$

Polynomials 10 (p. 15)

a. $3x^3 + 3x^2 - 7x + 1$
b. $-7a^3 + 4a^2 - 4a + 5$

Polynomials 11 (p. 16)

a. $4e^3 - 2e^2 + 4e + 8$
b. $6b^3 + 2b^2 + 7b - 15$

Polynomials 12 (p. 16)

a. $-r^3 - 3r^2 + 5r - 13$ b. $2y^4 - 3y$

Polynomials 13 (p. 16)

a. $2x + 8y - 5z$ b. $10a + b + 7$

Polynomials 14 (p. 16)

$5n + 10$

Polynomials 15 (p. 16)

a. $-20b^9$ b. $12x^3y + 6x^2y^2 - 3x^2yr$
c. $7m^5 - 21m^6 + 35m^4$

Polynomials 16 (p. 17)

a. $x^2 - 3x - 40$ b. $18a^2 + 3a - 10$
c. $8p^2 - 10pr - 3r^2$

Polynomials 17 (p. 17)

a. $4n^2 - 12nm + 9m^2$ b. $y^3 - 3y^2 - 9y - 5$
c. $d^3 - 6d^2 + 12d - 8$

Polynomials 18 (p. 17)

a. $g^2 - 25$ b. $4a^2 - 4ab + b^2$
c. $16h^{10} - 9i^8$

Polynomials 19 (p. 17)

a. $4r^2 - 2r + 3$ b. $6a^3 - 3a + 2$
c. $4n^4 + 2n^2 - 3n + 1$

Polynomials 20 (p. 17)

a. $2c + 1$ b. $2y - 5$ c. $3x + 4$

Factoring 1 (p. 18)

a. 2^4 b. $3^2 \cdot 5^3$ c. $2 \cdot 5 \cdot 3^3$
d. $11^5 \cdot 13^2$

Factoring 2 (p. 18)

a. $2 \cdot 5 \cdot 7$ b. $3^3 \cdot 5$ c. $2 \cdot 13^2$
d. $2^3 \cdot 5^3$

Factoring 3 (p. 18)

a. $3(p + 5)$ b. $r(2 + 7r)$
c. $4(4x + 3y)$ or $2(8x + 6y)$
d. $4b(b - 2)$ or $2b(2b - 4)$

Factoring 4 (p. 18)
a. $2m^2n(m - 6n^3)$ b. $5x^2y(1 - 3xy^2)$
c. $4gh(g + 2gh + 3)$

Factoring 5 (p. 18)
a. $9a^2b^3(b - 6a^3)$ b. $2x(x^2 - 3x + 5)$
c. $-5c^2d^4(3c + 7c^2d + 11)$

Factoring 6 (p. 19)
a. $(x + 1)(x + 11)$ b. $(3 + c)(16 + c)$
c. $(m - 2)(m - 7)$ d. $(b - 2)(b - 16)$

Factoring 7 (p. 19)
a. $(y + 1)(y + 3)$ b. $(1 + j)(7 + j)$
c. $(k + 1)(k + 13)$ d. $(s - 5)(s - 7)$

Factoring 8 (p. 19)
a. $(x - 4y)(x - 12y)$ b. $(r - 3s)(r - 24s)$
c. $(u^2 - 2)(u^2 - 14)$ d. $(a + 2b)(a + 30b)$

Factoring 9 (p. 19)
a. $(y - 4)(y + 3)$ b. $(x + 7)(x - 1)$
c. $(b + 3)(b - 1)$ d. $(r - 15)(r + 2)$

Factoring 10 (p. 19)
a. $(a - 2b)(a + b)$ b. $(m - 16n)(m + 2n)$
c. $(x - 10y)(x + 2y)$ d. $(r^2 - 25)(r^2 + 2)$

Factoring 11 (p. 20)
a. $(3a + 2)(a - 8)$ b. $(2b + 5)(b + 1)$
c. $(3x + 5)(x + 4)$ d. $(5y + 2)(y - 3)$

Factoring 12 (p. 20)
a. $(m - 6)^2$ b. $(t + 10)^2$
c. $(x + 4)^2$ d. $(r + 13)^2$

Factoring 13 (p. 20)
a. $(5a + 1)^2$ b. $(7c + 1)^2$
c. $mn(n^2 - m^2)$ d. $(3h^6 + 1)^2$

Factoring 14 (p. 20)
a. $3x(5x + 4 + 2x^2)$ b. $4(y - 3)$
c. $36(a - b)$ d. $(m + n)(r + s)$

Factoring 15 (p. 20)
a. $(y - 5)(y + 5 + x)$ b. $(b + c)(a - 3)$
c. $(p - 2)(m + 3n)$ d. $(q - 2)(2p - 5r)$

Factoring 16 (p. 21)
a. $n = 0, -4$ b. $p = 0, 2$ c. $h = 0, -3$

Factoring 17 (p. 21)
a. $a = 5, 3$ b. $r = 6, -3$ c. $b = -8, \frac{3}{2}$

Factoring 18 (p. 21)
a. $x = 3$ b. $a = 0, -\frac{3}{5}, \frac{7}{2}$
c. $y = 0, -3, 3, -1, 1$

Factoring 19 (p. 21)
$n(n + 1) = 56$; $n = 7$ or -8
The two integers are 7 and 8 or -7 and -8.

Factoring 20 (p. 21)
a. $b = 0, 3$ b. $c = 3, -6$ c. $y = \frac{3}{4}, -5$

Rational Expressions 1 (p. 22)
a. 2   b. $5, \frac{2}{3}$ c. $-\frac{1}{2}$ d. -4, 4

Rational Expressions 2 (p. 22)
a. $\dfrac{1}{4a}$, $a \neq 0$ b. $7, x \neq 2$

c. $\dfrac{1}{5r - 2}$, $r \neq \frac{3}{5}, 2$ d. $\dfrac{4y + 3}{6}$ There is no value where the expression is undefined.

Rational Expressions 3 (p. 22)
a. $\dfrac{2y - 1}{y + 5}$, $y \neq -5$ b. $\dfrac{2z + 9}{z - 11}$, $z \neq 11, -1$

Rational Expressions 4 (p. 22)
a. $\dfrac{20}{3s^3y}$ b. $\dfrac{4x}{yz}$ c. $\dfrac{n + 2}{n + 5}$

Rational Expressions 5 (p. 22)
a. $\frac{1}{2}$ b. $\dfrac{y - 5}{3y - 4}$ c. 1

Rational Expressions 6 (p. 23)
a. $-\dfrac{3m + 2}{m}$ b. $\dfrac{b + 2}{b - 2}$

Rational Expressions 7 (p. 23)

a. $\dfrac{4}{3y}$ b. $\dfrac{a^4}{b^3}$ c. $\dfrac{12}{r}$

Rational Expressions 8 (p. 23)

a. $\dfrac{3x}{7y}$ b. $\dfrac{1}{c+14}$ c. $\dfrac{s+3}{s+4}$

Rational Expressions 9 (p. 23)

a. $\dfrac{5(2e-5)}{e-5}$ b. $\dfrac{a+3}{a-5}$

Rational Expressions 10 (p. 23)

a. $6a^3b^5$ b. $60x^3y^2$

Rational Expressions 11 (p. 24)

a. $10mn$ b. $(d+2)(d-2)$

Rational Expressions 12 (p. 24)

a. $9x^2y^2$ b. $\dfrac{5y}{9x^2y^2}$ $\dfrac{6x^3}{9x^2y^2}$

Rational Expressions 13 (p. 24)

a. $\dfrac{6}{b}$ b. $\dfrac{7p}{p+1}$ c. 4

Rational Expressions 14 (p. 24)

a. $\dfrac{24}{(5-b)(b+5)}$ b. $\dfrac{c+1}{2c^2}$ c. $\dfrac{10-y}{5(y+4)}$

Rational Expressions 15 (p. 24)

a. $\dfrac{r-3}{6r^3}$ b. $\dfrac{m^2-m+10}{(m+2)(m-6)}$ c. $\dfrac{u+2}{u-4}$

Rational Expressions 16 (p. 25)

a. $\dfrac{2e+1}{e}$ b. $\dfrac{5y-7}{y}$ c. $\dfrac{3i^2-i-1}{i}$

Rational Expressions 17 (p. 25)

a. $\dfrac{a^2+4a-1}{a+2}$ b. $\dfrac{k}{k+4}$

Rational Expressions 18 (p. 25)

a. yes   b. no   c. no   d. yes

Rational Expressions 19 (p. 25)

a. 36   b. 5   c. 0

Rational Expressions 20 (p. 25)

a. $\frac{10}{23}$ b. $\frac{13}{23}$ c. $\frac{19}{23}$

Linear Equations and Inequalities in Two Variables 1 (p. 26)

a. yes   b. no   c. yes   d. yes
e. no

Linear Equations and Inequalities in Two Variables 2 (p. 26)

a. B   b. D
c. A   d. C

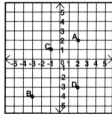

Linear Equations and Inequalities in Two Variables 3 (p. 26)

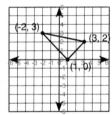

Linear Equations and Inequalities in Two Variables 4 (p. 26)

Table will vary.

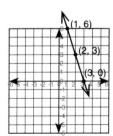

Linear Equations and Inequalities in Two Variables 5 (p. 26)

a. 6   b. 8   c. -6   d. -2

Linear Equations and Inequalities in Two Variables 6 (p. 27)

x intercept: 7   4   2

y intercept: 7   8   -6

Linear Equations and Inequalities in Two Variables 7 (p. 27)

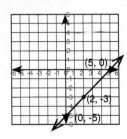

Linear Equations and Inequalities in Two Variables 8 (p. 27)

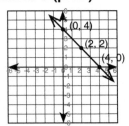

Linear Equations and Inequalities in Two Variables 9 (p. 27)

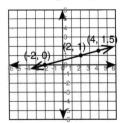

Linear Equations and Inequalities in Two Variables 10 (p. 27)

a. $y = 8 - x$ b. $y = \dfrac{4x + 1}{2}$ c. $y = \dfrac{3x - 35}{4}$

Linear Equations and Inequalities in Two Variables 11 (p. 28)

a. $-\frac{1}{2}$ b. $\frac{4}{5}$ c. $\frac{1}{3}$

Linear Equations and Inequalities in Two Variables 12 (p. 28)

a. 0   b. -5   c. 2

Linear Equations and Inequalities in Two Variables 13 (p. 28)

$x = 1$

Linear Equations and Inequalities in Two Variables 14 (p. 28)

slope = $-\frac{4}{3}$ y intercept = 4

Linear Equations and Inequalities in Two Variables 15 (p. 28)

slope = 8 y intercept = -2

Linear Equations and Inequalities in Two Variables 16 (p. 29)

$y = 3x - 9$

Linear Equations and Inequalities in Two Variables 17 (p. 29)

$x + 2y = 6$

Linear Equations and Inequalities in Two Variables 18 (p. 29)

$-3x + 2y = 6$

Linear Equations and Inequalities in Two Variables 19 (p. 29)

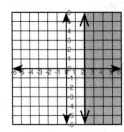

Linear Equations and Inequalities in Two Variables 20 (p. 29)

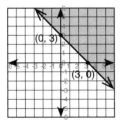

Systems of Linear Equations and Inequalities 1 (p. 30)

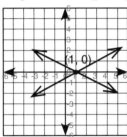

Systems of Linear Equations and Inequalities 2 (p. 30)

intersecting lines; one solution

Systems of Linear Equations and Inequalities 3 (p. 30)

a. (7, 14)   b. (5, -2)

Systems of Linear Equations and Inequalities 4 (p. 30)

a. (2, -1)   b. $(\frac{2}{3}, 3)$

Systems of Linear Equations and Inequalities 5 (p. 30)

a. (1, 1)   b. (3, 0)

Systems of Linear Equations and Inequalities 6 (p. 31)

a. (11, -1)   b. (2, 6)

Systems of Linear Equations and Inequalities 7 (p. 31)

a. (-3, 3)   b. (3, 1)

Systems of Linear Equations and Inequalities 8 (p. 31)

a. (1, 1)   b. (-4, -5)

Systems of Linear Equations and Inequalities 9 (p. 31)

a. $n = 2m + 4$ b. $a = \frac{1}{2}(b - 3)$

Systems of Linear Equations and Inequalities 10 (p. 31)

a. $S + 6 = 2R + 4$ b. $0.10d = \dfrac{0.25q}{2}$

Systems of Linear Equations and Inequalities 11 (p. 32)

a. $\begin{cases} 5n + 25q = 310 \\ n + q = 26 \end{cases}$ 17 nickels, 9 quarters

Systems of Linear Equations and Inequalities 12 (p. 32)

a. $\begin{cases} x + y = 36 \\ x - y = 4 \end{cases}$ (20, 16)

Systems of Linear Equations and Inequalities 13 (p. 32)

a. $\begin{cases} J + D = 137 \\ J = 2D - 10 \end{cases}$ José 88, Dan 49

Systems of Linear Equations and Inequalities 14 (p. 32)

a. $\begin{cases} E = M + 3 \\ E - 4 = 2(M - 4) \end{cases}$ Ella 10, Marta 7

Systems of Linear Equations and Inequalities 15 (p. 32)

a. $\begin{cases} D = 3A \\ (D + 3) + (A + 3) = 54 \end{cases}$ David 36, Alex 12

Square Roots and Radicals 1 (p. 33)

a. 7   b. ±0.9   c. $-\frac{1}{4}$ d. 30

Square Roots and Radicals 2 (p. 33)

a. ±24   b. 0.05   c. -3   d. -1.4

Square Roots and Radicals 3 (p. 33)

a. 3   b. 2   c. 4   d. -5

Square Roots and Radicals 4 (p. 33)
a. $6\sqrt{2}$ b. $6\sqrt{3}$ c. $2\sqrt{11}$ d. $3\sqrt{10}$

Square Roots and Radicals 5 (p. 33)
a. $2\sqrt{6}$ b. $5\sqrt{6}$ c. $4\sqrt{3}$ d. $10\sqrt{10}$

Square Roots and Radicals 6 (p. 34)
a. $2\sqrt{2}$ b. $2\sqrt{7}$ c. $3\sqrt{3}$

Square Roots and Radicals 7 (p. 34)
a. $3ab^2\sqrt{a}$ b. $\dfrac{5\sqrt{2}}{7}$ c. $\dfrac{9\sqrt{5}}{5}$ d. $\frac{5}{9}$

Square Roots and Radicals 8 (p. 34)
a. $7\sqrt{11}$ b. $4\sqrt{15}$ c. $-3\sqrt{6}$

Square Roots and Radicals 9 (p. 34)
a. $-2\sqrt{x}$ b. $3\sqrt{r}$ c. $23\sqrt{3}$

Square Roots and Radicals 10 (p. 34)
a. $x^2\sqrt{y}$ b. $9y^4\sqrt{y}$ c. b^2c^3 d. $2r^2\sqrt{22}$

Square Roots and Radicals 11 (p. 35)
a. $19\sqrt{5}$ b. $4\sqrt{n}$

Square Roots and Radicals 12 (p. 35)
a. $12\sqrt{y}$ b. 0

Square Roots and Radicals 13 (p. 35)
a. $5\sqrt{2}$ b. $-6\sqrt{6}$ c. $\sqrt{3}$

Square Roots and Radicals 14 (p. 35)
a. -7   b. $4\sqrt{7}+7$ c. $16n$

Square Roots and Radicals 15 (p. 35)
a. $\dfrac{\sqrt{2}}{2}$ b. $-\frac{2}{5}\sqrt{15}$ c. $\frac{3}{16}$

Square Roots and Radicals 16 (p. 36)
a. $\dfrac{\sqrt{6}}{2}$ b. $\dfrac{2\sqrt{2y}}{y}$ c. $2x$

Square Roots and Radicals 17 (p. 36)
a. 64   b. 12   c. $\frac{17}{2}$

Square Roots and Radicals 18 (p. 36)
a. 11   b. 6   c. 27

Square Roots and Radicals 19 (p. 36)
a. $b=12$ b. $a=3$ c. $c=2$

Square Roots and Radicals 20 (p. 36)
a. 5   b. 10

Quadratic Equations 1 (p. 37)
a. (4, -3)   b. $(0, \frac{9}{4})$ c. $(\frac{3}{2}, \frac{4}{3})$

Quadratic Equations 2 (p. 37)
a. $(-\frac{2}{3}, 5)$ b. $(0, \frac{12}{7})$ c. $(-3, \frac{2}{5})$

Quadratic Equations 3 (p. 37)
a. $\pm\dfrac{\sqrt{10}}{5}$ b. $\pm\dfrac{\sqrt{2}}{2}$ c. $\pm 2\sqrt{2}$

Quadratic Equations 4 (p. 37)
a. $g=\pm 7$ b. $h=\pm 13$ c. $x=\pm\frac{9}{5}$

Quadratic Equations 5 (p. 37)
a. (4, -2)   b. $\pm 2\sqrt{3}$ c. $(-1, \frac{1}{7})$

Quadratic Equations 6 (p. 38)
a. (-2, 4)   b. $-5\pm\sqrt{22}$ c. $\frac{3}{2}$

Quadratic Equations 7 (p. 38)
a. $\dfrac{1\pm\sqrt{5}}{2}$ b. (-15, 3)   c. $2\pm\sqrt{2}$

Quadratic Equations 8 (p. 39)
a. $(-1, \frac{5}{2})$ b. (-3, -2)

Quadratic Equations 9 (p. 39)
a. (5, -2)   b. (2, 1)

Quadratic Equations 10 (p. 39)
a. $\pm\sqrt{5}$ b. (3, 1)